A Beginning-to-Read Book

A New Home

by Mary Lindeen

NORWOODHOUSE PRESS

DEAR CAREGIVER, The *Beginning to Read—Read and Discover* books provide emergent reader the opportunity to explore the world through nonfiction while building early reading skills. The text integrates bo common sight words and content vocabulary. These key words are featured on lists provided at the back of the book to help your child expand his or her sight word recognition, which helps build reading fluency. The conte words expand vocabulary and support comprehension.

Nonfiction text is any text that is factual. The Common Core State Standards call for an increase in the amo of informational text reading among students. The Standards aim to promote college and career readiness amo students. Preparation for college and career endeavors requires proficiency in reading complex informational te in a variety of content areas. You can help your child build a foundation by introducing nonfiction early. To furth support the CCSS, you will find Reading Reinforcement activities at the back of the book that are aligned to the Standards.

Above all, the most important part of the reading experience is to have fun and enjoy it!

Sincerely,

Shannon Cannon

Shannon Cannon, Ph.D.
Literacy Consultant

Norwood House Press
For more information about Norwood House Press please visit our website at
www.norwoodhousepress.com or call 866-565-2900.
© 2022 Norwood House Press. Beginning-to-Read™ is a trademark of Norwood House Press.
All rights reserved. No part of this book may be reproduced or utilized in any form or by any
means without written permission from the publisher.

Editor: Judy Kentor Schmauss
Designer: Sara Radka

Photo Credits:
All images sourced from Getty Images.

Library of Congress Cataloging-in-Publication Data
Names: Lindeen, Mary, author.
Title: A new home / by Mary Lindeen.
Description: Chicago : Norwood House Press, 2022. | Series: A beginning-to-read book | Audience:
    Grades K-1 | Summary: "Describes what happens when people move to a new home, including
    how their belongings get from one place to another and their opportunities for new experiences in a
    new place. This title includes a note to caregivers, reading activities, and a word list. An early social
    and emotional book that includes reading activities and a word list"– Provided by publisher.
Identifiers: LCCN 2021049737 (print) | LCCN 2021049738 (ebook) | ISBN 9781684507887
    (hardcover) | ISBN 9781684047345 (paperback) | ISBN 9781684047383 (epub)
Subjects: LCSH: Moving, Household–Juvenile literature. | Home–Juvenile literature.
Classification: LCC TX307 .L56 2022 (print) | LCC TX307 (ebook) | DDC 648/.9–dc23/eng/20211109
LC record available at https://lccn.loc.gov/2021049737
LC ebook record available at https://lccn.loc.gov/2021049738

Hardcover ISBN: 978-1-68450-788-7
Paperback ISBN: 978-1-68404-734-5

It's moving day!

It's time to go to a new home.

Clothes and toys are in boxes.

Dishes and books are in boxes.

Lots of things are in boxes.

But some things are too big for boxes!

Everything gets
loaded into
a big truck.

The truck is called
a moving van.

The new home
is empty at first.

It's fun to look
around and
explore.

Then the moving van comes!

Everything gets unloaded from the truck.

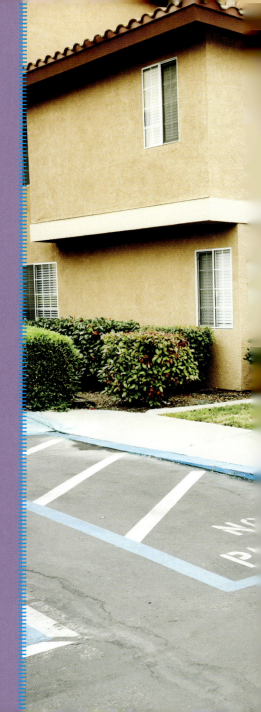

All the boxes
get carried in.

Now it's time
to unpack.

Everything
gets put in
the right spot.

New neighbors come to welcome you.

It's good to meet them!

Sometimes they bring a gift.

They are happy to have new neighbors.

It can be hard to leave your old home.

But it can also be exciting to move to a new home.

There are lots
of things to
learn about in
a new home.

It has new
rooms to live in.

There are new places for taking walks.

There are new places to play.

And there are
new friends
to play with!

...READING REINFORCEMENT...

CRAFT AND STRUCTURE

To check your child's understanding of the organization of the book, recreate the following chart on a sheet of paper. Ask your child to complete the chart by writing things you do before you move and things you do after you move:

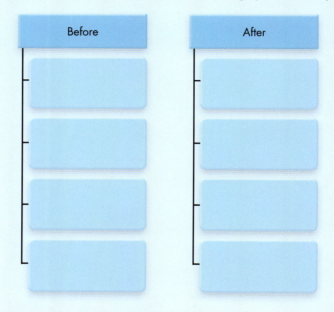

Before	After

VOCABULARY: Learning Content Words

Content words are words that are specific to a particular topic. All the content words in this book can be found on page 32. Use some or all of these content words to complete one or more of the following activities:

1. Give your child three clues about a word and have them guess it.

2. Help your child name synonyms and antonyms for the words.

3. Say a sentence but omit the word. Have your child guess the missing word.

4. Say one of the words. Have your child say the first word that comes to mind.

5. Have your child sort the words into categories. Then have them tell you how they sorted the words.

FOUNDATIONAL SKILLS: Multisyllabic Words

Every syllable in a word has a vowel sound. Have your child clap out the syllables and tell how many there are in each word below. Then help your child find words with more than one syllable in this book.

frog	elephant	home
bathtub	apple	porcupine

CLOSE READING OF INFORMATIONAL TEXT

Close reading helps children comprehend text. It includes reading a text, discussing it with others, and answering questions about it. Use these questions to discuss this book with your child:

1. What are the kids doing on page 3?
2. How do you think kids can help with packing and unpacking?
3. What's one good thing about moving? One bad thing?
4. Why do you think people put things in boxes when they move?
5. How did you feel when you moved? If you haven't moved before, how do you think you would feel?

FLUENCY

Fluency is the ability to read accurately with speed and expression. Help your child practice fluency by using one or more of the following activities:

1. Reread the book to your child at least two times while he or she uses a finger to track each word as it is read.
2. Read a line of the book, then reread it as your child reads along with you.
3. Ask your child to go back through the book and read the words he or she knows.
4. Have your child practice reading the book several times to improve accuracy, rate, and expression.

••• Word List •••

A New Home uses the 85 words listed below. *High-frequency words* are those words that are use
most often in the English language. They are sometimes referred to as *sight words* because childre
need to learn to recognize them automatically when they read. *Content words* are any words speci
to a particular topic. Regular practice reading these words will enhance your child's ability to read w
greater fluency and comprehension.

High-Frequency Words

a	called	have	place(s)	things
about	can	home	play	time
all	come(s)	in	put	to
also	day	into	right	too
and	first	is	some	with
are	for	it	take(ing)	you
around	from	look	the	your
at	get(s)	new	them	
be	go	now	then	
big	good	of	there	
but	has	old	they	

Content Words

books	everything	hard	meet	truck
boxes	exciting	it's	move(ing)	unloaded
bring	explore	learn	neighbors	unpack
carried	friends	leave	rooms	van
clothes	fun	live	sometimes	walks
dishes	gift	loaded	spot	welcome
empty	happy	lots	toys	

••• About the Author

Mary Lindeen is a writer, editor, parent, and former elementary school teacher.
She has written more than 100 books for children and edited many more.
She specializes in early literacy instruction and books for young readers,
especially nonfiction.